COOK QUICKLY – EAT ENJOYABLY

Start with the shopping

What is the point of cooking quickly if you have already had to waste a lot of time shopping? To avoid this, it is worthwhile spending a little time on planning your shopping and keeping a check on store-cupboard ingredients.

Check your store-cupboard:
• Whenever you run out of something or your stock gets low, write it down.
• Divide your shopping list up into shops or sections of the supermarket.
• Try to shop only once a month for long-lasting items, such as jam, dry goods and drinks.
• If possible, buy home-grown fresh fruit and vegetables. Their quality is best and they are at their least expensive when they are in season.
• Buy meat and fish fresh and either use them at once or freeze them.
• Buy frozen foods at the end of your shopping trip and pack them in freezer bags.

Keep fresh food fresh

Nearly all foodstuffs are marked with a use-by date to guide you. Fresh foods should, of course, be used as soon after purchase as possible because they taste better and retain many valuable nutrients.

Leafy vegetables, such as lettuce and spinach, will keep for four days, unwashed and loosely wrapped in newspaper in the refrigerator. Alternatively, you can wash them at once and store in a plastic container in the vegetable compartment of the refrigerator. This may be more convenient, as you can always take out the quantity you actually need.

Herbs should not be put in water or they will wilt more rapidly. Wrap them in newspaper and store in the salad drawer of the refrigerator.

Firm vegetables, such as cauliflower, courgettes and carrots, will keep for about seven days in the salad drawer of the refrigerator. Do not put tomatoes into the refrigerator, as they will lose their taste.

Onions and garlic can be stored at room temperature. In winter, garlic may grow a green shoot. Removed this, as it produces a bitter taste.

Most kinds of fruit can be stored for up to seven days at room temperature. Berries of all kinds are particularly sensitive. Always remove them immediately from their packaging and put them on a plate in a single layer. Keep them for a maximum of two days. Citrus fruits should not be stored in the refrigerator, as they lose their aroma.

Meat and poultry should always be removed immediately from their wrapping. Put them into an earthenware or glass dish and keep them in the refrigerator for a maximum of two days. If you brush a mixture of oil and herbs on to steaks and chops, they will keep for three days and will also be very tender. Minced meat absolutely must be used the same day. Sausages should be stored in an airtight container in the refrigerator. Use within three or four days of purchase.

Fresh fish is best used on the day it is bought, if possible, but it may be stored, loosely wrapped in greaseproof paper in the refrigerator, for no more than one day. Otherwise, it is better to freeze it. Fresh seafood, such as crab, prawns and mussels, should always be used on the day of purchase.

Use only very fresh eggs. They must be stored in the refrigerator and can keep for up to two weeks. To tell if an egg is fresh, put it in a bowl of water. If it sinks to the bottom, it is fresh. If the blunt end tips upwards, it should be used soon. If it stands vertically in the water, it should not be used. Never store eggs near strong-smelling foods, as they quickly pick up the smell.

Fats and oils should be stored well-sealed, because they quickly pick up outside smells.

Butter and other spreading fats should be stored in the refrigerator. Take note of their use-by date.

Dairy products should be stored in the refrigerator and should not be used after their use-by date. Ultra-high-heat

(UHT) milk products can be stored unopened and unrefrigerated – ideal for the store cupboard. Cheese, apart from soft cheeses, which should be eaten within a maximum of two days of purchase, should be stored in the refrigerator.

Sensible supplies for lightning meals

From the refrigerator

Full-fat cream cheese is a real quick-change artist:
• As an exquisite starter: mix it with finely chopped ham, smoked pork or smoked fish. Use two tablespoons to shape the mixture into dumplings. Arrange the cream cheese dumplings with a bright mixed salad on individual plates.
• As a sharp sauce: mix the cream cheese with a little meat or vegetable stock and then pep it up with wine, passata, stoned olives or chopped fresh herbs. It goes well with stir-fried meat, fish or pasta.
• For a sweet variation: mix it with puréed berries, reserving some whole berries for garnish. You can spread the mixture on to a biscuit base, pre-soaked with brandy, liqueur or fruit juice. Garnish with fresh fruits and your lightning cake is ready for surprise guests.

Quark or other curd cheese
• Mix it with freshly chopped herbs, onions and diced tomatoes and season to taste with salt and pepper. Stuff

chicory leaves or scooped-out tomatoes with the mixture, simply serve it with crusty fresh bread or use as a topping for boiled potatoes.
• As a dessert: mix it with desiccated coconut and rum, with rum and raisins or with fruit or fruit purée, according to taste.

Slicing or grating cheese
• Lightning toast: spread a slice of bread with butter. Place a slice of ham or salami and some sliced tomato on it. Top with grated or sliced cheese and toast in a preheated oven at 200°C/400°F/ Gas 6 or under a preheated grill for about 8 minutes, until the cheese has melted.
• Cheese salad: finely dice some cheese and mix it with cold, diced boiled potatoes, chopped onions and herbs and serve with an oil and white wine vinegar dressing mixed with a little mustard.
• Pizza: spread chopped canned tomatoes or tomato purée on a ready-made pizza base. Arrange slices of mozzarella, salami and sliced peppers on top and finish with a layer of grated Parmesan cheese. Bake in a preheated oven at 200°C/400°F/ Gas 6 for about 20 minutes.

Instant and ready-made desserts
• Mix a vanilla or chocolate dessert with beaten double cream and sprinkle it with roasted sesame seeds.
• Mix the dessert with ground hazelnuts, fill ready-made short

crust pastry tart cases with the mixture and sprinkle fresh berries on top.
• Mix the dessert with grated coconut and pieces of fruit.

From the freezer

Vegetables
• Spinach soup: cook chopped thawed spinach in chicken, beef or vegetable stock, mix it with crème fraîche or soured cream, add a few thawed prawns and heat through.
• Pea soup or hotpot: cook frozen peas in beef, ham or vegetable stock and then purée them with a hand-held electric mixer. Stir in some cream and season to taste with salt and pepper. You can add some finely chopped Kabanos sausage, diced potato and diced vegetables to this basic soup to produce a satisfying hotpot. Alternatively, you can embellish the basic soup with strips of leek.
• Minestrone: cook a mixture of diced vegetables in beef, chicken or vegetable stock. Sprinkle with freshly grated Parmesan cheese and serve with French bread.
• Vegetable salad: blanch a mixture of diced vegetables for 3–4 minutes, then strain. Mix together white wine vinegar, olive oil and finely chopped herbs and toss the vegetables in the dressing.
• Spinach with cheese topping: briefly cook some thawed leaf spinach with 1 crushed garlic clove. Mix it with bacon strips, roast chicken breast, turkey strips or tiger prawns and pine

kernels, sprinkle with grated cheese and bake in a preheated oven at 180°C/350°F/Gas 4 for about 15 minutes. Alternatively, cook it in the microwave on HIGH for about 10 minutes. This dish also tastes good made with peas, broccoli, leeks or diced mixed vegetables.
• Vegetable omelette: beat an egg yolk and mix it with some diced mixed vegetables and a pinch of finely chopped herbs. Beat the egg white with a pinch of salt until stiff and fold it into the egg yolk mixture. Fry the omelette in a little oil until it is golden yellow on both sides.
• Vegetable flan: mix together diced mixed vegetables, eggs and grated cheese. Roll out some thawed ready-made pastry and place it into a loose-based flan tin. Spread the vegetable mixture on top. Bake the flan in a preheated oven at 200°C/400°F/Gas 6 for about 25 minutes. Serve with a mixed salad or a sauce made of yogurt, crème fraîche, herbs and garlic. This flan also tastes good made with green beans or other vegetables.
• Potato cakes: fry them and serve with 5 ml/1 teaspoon caviar and 15 ml/1 tablespoon crème fraîche .
• Potato croquettes: serve with herby crème fraîche and strips of smoked salmon or with herby Quark.

Fish and meat
• Fish soup: thaw some plaice fillets and cut them into bite-size pieces. Heat together some fish stock and white wine. Add the pieces of plaice

and some peas and simmer until they are cooked. Sprinkle with dill and serve.

Frozen pastry
• You can create bacon or cheese horns with thawed frozen puff pastry. Roll out the pastry and cut it into triangles. Sprinkle them with grated cheese or diced bacon, roll them up and brush them with beaten egg. Bake them in a preheated oven at 200°C/400°F/Gas 6 for about 10–12 minutes, until they are crisp and golden.
• Puff pastry horns also taste good with sweet fillings, such as finely chopped marzipan, chocolate or chopped nuts and dried fruits.

Berries and ice cream
• Purée some thawed berries and serve as a hot or cold fruit sauce with ice cream.
• For an imaginative cocktail, rub thawed, puréed berries through a strainer with the back of a wooden spoon. Pour some champagne or sparkling wine on to 15 ml/1 tablespoon of the berry purée.
• Slice a fresh mango and serve with a scoop of ice cream. Sprinkle with grated coconut or chocolate.
• Fill ready-made chocolate cups with ice cream and sprinkle with finely chopped pistachio nuts.
• Cut a melon in half and remove the seeds. Scoop out the flesh with a melon-baller. Fill the melon shells with ice cream, garnish with mint sprigs and serve with the melon.

From the store cupboard

Juices and stock You should always have juices and stock cubes or granules in your store cupboard, so that you can easily make a soup or sauce in a matter of minutes.
• Vegetable soup: heat some vegetable juice or stock and add grated carrots, courgettes and celery. This also works very well with frozen mixed vegetables.
• Chicken soup: heat some vegetable juice or chicken stock. Cook rice, peas and thin strips of boneless, skinless chicken breast in it. Sprinkle with chopped parsley.
• Soup with dumplings: heat some beef stock and cook dumplings made of sausage meat in it. Garnish with snipped chives.
• Prawn soup: heat some fish stock with cream and white wine. Warm a few prawns in it and garnish with dill.

Tomatoes Whether canned whole or chopped, tomato purée or passata, that is, sieved, with or without herbs – tomatoes are extremely versatile and always useful for a quick meal.
• Tomato soup: mix some passata with a little lemon juice and 45–60 ml/3–4 tablespoons pesto and heat. Instead of pesto, you can use whipped cream. If necessary, you can thin the soup with a little water or stock and season it with salt and pepper. Sprinkle with toasted slivered almonds or with croûtons.

• Pasta sauce: chop some fresh or canned tomatoes or use tomato purée. Heat the tomatoes with cream and mix with torn fresh basil leaves. Alternatively, mix them with fried minced beef, chopped canned tuna, capers or olives.

Canned pulses Lentils, chickpeas, and all kinds of beans can be used for:
• Salad: mix pulses with crumbled ewe's milk cheese and onions or garlic and serve with a dressing of oil, white wine vinegar and chopped fresh herbs.

• Dip: purée some pulses and mix them with a little oil, garlic, salt and pepper. This dip goes well with grilled fish, fondue or on rustic bread.
• Hotpot: cook a mixture of pulses with fried diced bacon or smoked sausage in stock. Season if necessary.
• Bean hotpot: fry some minced beef with chopped onions and add tomato purée or passata. Season well with salt, black pepper and cayenne pepper, add mixed beans and heat through.
• Dried yellow or red lentils cook quickly and can be used

like other pulses. They also taste delicious with chopped turkey or chicken breast.

Vegetables, canned or bottled
• Sauerkraut salad: chop some canned sauerkraut. Mix it with diced apple and fried diced bacon and serve with a vinaigrette dressing.
• Salad with sweetcorn and artichoke hearts: serve them with lettuce or mixed salad leaves and toss in a dressing made of white wine vinegar, oil, mustard, salt and pepper.
• Beetroot salad: mix the beetroot with finely chopped

Convenience foods are ideal if you are in a hurry. With a little imagination and not much expense, you can conjure up delicious dishes in a flash. You will find some suggestions on pages 5, 6, 7 and 8.

onions, herbs and walnuts and serve with a vinaigrette or soured cream dressing.
• Red cabbage hotpot: cook some red cabbage in stock. Heat some leftover roast game, turkey, duck or ham in it and stir in some soured cream.
• Beetroot sauce: purée some beetroot and mix it with whipped cream. This goes well with fried or grilled fish.
• Beetroot soup: purée some beetroot and bring to the boil in chicken or vegetable stock. Season to taste and serve with a swirl of whipped cream and chopped fresh herbs.

Pasta and rice
• Pasta with cheese topping: mix together cooked, drained pasta with diced continental sausage and put it into an ovenproof dish. Beat some eggs, stir in grated cheese and spread the mixture over the pasta. Bake for 15–20 minutes in a preheated oven at 200°C/ 400°F/Gas 6.
• Pasta with ham: sauté some cooked drained pasta with diced ham and finely chopped spring onions in a little oil. Beat some eggs, season with salt and pepper, pour them over the pasta and cook until just set.
• Fried rice: fry some boiled, well-drained rice with peas, diced tomatoes and canned tuna in a pan with little oil, stirring constantly. Season with salt and pepper.
• Rice salad: mix some boiled, drained rice with prawns and drained canned sweetcorn. Then mix in plenty of chopped fresh parsley and a dressing of

white wine vinegar, olive oil, salt and pepper.

Mashed potato
• Potato soup: prepare some instant mash potato following the instructions on the packet. Add enough beef, chicken or vegetable stock to turn the purée into a thick soup. If liked, stir in some cream. Depending on your taste, add prawns, herbs, strips of smoked salmon, diced vegetables or ham.
• Potato pie: make some instant mash potato following the instructions on the packet. Mix it with liver sausage and sauerkraut. Put it into an ovenproof dish, sprinkle with grated cheese and bake in a preheated oven at 200°C/ 400°F/Gas 6 for about 30 minutes.

Canned fish
• Tuna dip: purée some tuna. Mix it with garlic, tomato purée and herbs. Spread it on thick rustic bread, or use to fill little pastry cases or to stuff scooped-out tomatoes.
• Tuna pizza: place some rolled out pizza dough on a baking sheet. Spread tomatoes and sliced mozzarella cheese over it and top with tuna. Bake in a preheated oven at 200°C/ 400°F/Gas 6 for about 20-25 minutes. The pizza also tastes good made with sardines or anchovies.
• Sardines in vinaigrette: sprinkle some sardines with a vinaigrette made of white wine vinegar, olive oil, garlic and lots of fresh herbs. Serve with fresh wholemeal toast.

Other useful store-cupboard items:
• Pickles, such as gherkins, pearl onions and mixed pickles
• Canned or packet soups
• Custard powder, instant desserts, jellies and blancmange
• Canned sausages and frankfurters
• Red and white wine vinegar
• Various cooking and salad oils
• Olives and capers
• Mayonnaise, mustard, creamed horseradish
• Tomato purée
• Dried mushrooms
• Spices, dried herbs and pesto
• Breadcrumbs, crispbread
• Plain, self-raising and wholemeal flour
• Honey and jam
• Nuts, desiccated coconut and seeds
• Onions, garlic and potatoes
• Lemons or lemon juice
• Sherry for sauces and soups, fruit liqueurs or fruit brandies for cakes and desserts

Save cooking time

• Think ahead. If you are cooking boiled potatoes for an evening meal, you can cook more potatoes than you need and use them next day for fried potatoes or a potato pie. The same applies to pasta or rice. They can be successfully re-heated in the microwave or by gentle steaming.
• When you are boiling potatoes, always choose small ones which are as equal in size as possible, so that they take the same time to cook.
• The smaller you chop the ingredients for a dish, the faster

they will cook. (This is the secret of stir-frying.)

• Chop vegetables directly into the saucepan. This reduces the amount of washing up.

• Use a swivel vegetable peeler to slice courgettes and carrots into thin strips. It looks attractive and the vegetables cook in no time at all.

• Put button and chestnut mushrooms into a strainer and rinse them briefly under running water, then shake them. This cleans them very quickly. Never immerse mushrooms in water because they soak it up. You can slice them with an egg slicer.

• Hard butter quickly becomes spreadable if you put it under a bowl which has been rinsed in hot water.

• Freeze Parmesan or other grating cheese in portions and use it when needed. You can grate the cheese while it is still frozen, which makes it particularly light.

• You can keep chopped onions mixed with a little oil and ready for use in a screw-top glass jar in the refrigerator.

• If you often use lemon juice and prefer it fresh, you can squeeze several fruits at once and keep the juice in a screw-top glass jar in the refrigerator.

• Make more salad dressing than you need and keep it in a screw-top glass jar. It will keep for 4–5 days in the refrigerator. Before using the dressing, shake it well. Add fresh herbs, onions or garlic just before using.

• Wash lettuce and drain it well. Store it in a plastic container in the refrigerator.

Useful equipment

Modern kitchen gadgets cannot take away all the work, but they can help or save you time.

Microwave: You can use it to thaw frozen or warm up cooked dishes and also to cook small portions more quickly. As well as this, microwave cooking is economical because you use little oil or liquid. Last but not least, you save on the washing up because you can serve the food in the microwave dishes. Crockery which can also be used for freezing is particularly practical. The microwave gives you good service if you:

• frequently cook small portions of vegetables

• are cooking pies or cheese-topped dishes (in this case, the microwave should also have a grill or browning facility).

• are cooking hotpots

• want to warm up a prepared side dish quickly

• are a fan of egg custards and flans, because you can make them successfully in the microwave without setting them over a pan of hot water and they cook more quickly.

Pressure cooker: It saves time in cooking vegetables, pulses (you do not have to soak them), frozen meat or stock. If possible, cook more than you need at one time and freeze the extra in portions.

Hand-held electric mixer: A purée attachment is ideal because you can easily purée soups, sauces, berries or

vegetables with it in the saucepan itself and this saves the washing up.

Lightning chopper: This gives good service if you want to chop onions, nuts, bread, cheese or herbs quickly. A food processor is a good, but more expensive alternative.

Universal slicer: This is indispensable for cutting vegetables into slices, matchsticks or flakes. There are models with different attachments, which are simple to use and clean. A food processor is a good, but more expensive alternative.

Also useful are:

• Good sharp knives. It is best if they are ready to hand in a knife holder or on a magnet. An efficient and safe knife sharpener is also invaluable.

• A large chopping board. Ideally, you should use separate boards for meat and vegetables and they should always be easy to scrub thoroughly clean.

• A garlic press.

• A pepper mill that works properly (many are more decorative than practical).

• A stable egg slicer (also for mushrooms, boiled potatoes and mozzarella cheese).

• Kitchen scissors for snipping chives, cress or other fresh herbs and bacon.

• A selection of strainers and a colander.

• Wooden spoons, a slotted spoon, tongs, a long-handled fork and a hand whisk.

• An easy-to-use can opener.

Tagliatelle with mushrooms

You can use any kind of flat ribbon pasta, such as fettuccine, for this recipe. Paglia e fieno – 'hay and straw' – a mixture of long green and yellow noodles would look particularly attractive.

Easy

Serves 2
150 g/5 oz dried green tagliatelle or
    other ribbon pasta
45 ml/3 tablespoons olive oil
1 onion
3 garlic cloves
250 g/9 oz oyster mushrooms
250 g/9 oz button mushrooms
5 ml/1 teaspoon thyme
75 ml/5 tablespoons dry
    white wine
150 ml/¹/4 pint crème fraîche
1 tablespoon tomato purée
1 bunch fresh parsley
salt and freshly ground black pepper
freshly grated Parmesan cheese,
    to serve

Approximately per portion:
2,900 kJ/690 kcal
21 g protein, 40 g fat
52 g carbohydrate

● Approximate preparation
time: 30 minutes

1. Bring a large saucepan of well-salted water to the boil. Add 15ml/1 tablespoon of the olive oil and the pasta. Bring back to the boil and cook for 10–12 minutes, until tender, but still firm to the bite. Tip the tagliatelle into a strainer and drain thoroughly.

2. Meanwhile, finely chop the onion and garlic. Tear the oyster mushrooms into smaller pieces and thinly slice the button mushrooms.

3. Heat the remaining olive oil in a frying pan. Add the onion and garlic and sauté over a low heat, stirring occasionally, until soft.

4. Add the mushrooms and fry over a medium heat for about 8 minutes, until nearly all the liquid has evaporated. Season with salt and pepper and stir in the thyme.

5. Stir in the white wine, crème fraîche and tomato purée and cook over a medium heat for a further 3 minutes.

6. Coarsely chop the parsley and mix with the mushrooms.

7. Put the drained tagliatelle in a warm serving bowl and pour the mushroom sauce on top. Toss thoroughly with 2 large forks to mix. Serve with the grated Parmesan cheese.

Ravioli in sage butter

For a special occasion

Serves 2
175 g/6 oz fresh ready-made ravioli
    or other filled pasta
1 shallot
1 garlic clove
40 g/1¹/2 oz butter
10 ml/2 teaspoons dried sage
30 ml/2 tablespoons freshly grated
    Parmesan cheese
salt and freshly ground pepper
tomato salad with basil, to serve

Approximately per portion:
2,200 kJ/520 kcal
16 g protein, 24 g fat
61 g carbohydrate

● Approximate preparation
time: 20 minutes

1. Bring a large saucepan of lightly salted water to the boil. Add the ravioli, bring back to the boil and cook for about 8 minutes, until tender, but still firm to the bite.

2. Finely chop the shallot and crush the garlic. Melt the butter in a saucepan. Add the shallot and garlic and sauté over a low heat, stirring occasionally, for about 5 minutes. Add the sage and season to taste with salt and pepper.

3. Thoroughly drain the ravioli. Arrange it on two individual warm plates and pour on the sage butter sauce. Finally, sprinkle the Parmesan cheese over it. Serve with tomato salad with basil.

Above: Ravioli in sage butter
Below: Tagliatelle with mushrooms

Egg salad with chicory

Easy

Serves 2
3 eggs
2 small heads chicory
1 bunch fresh dill
45 ml/3 tablespoons mayonnaise
45 ml/3 tablespoons white
    wine vinegar
15 ml/1 tablespoon olive oil
pinch of sugar
10 ml/2 teaspoons mild
    curry powder
salt and freshly ground white pepper
wholemeal bread and butter,
    to serve

Approximately per portion:
1,200 kJ/290 kcal
12 g protein, 25 g fat
5 g carbohydrate

● Approximate preparation
  time: 15 minutes

---

1. Cook the eggs in boiling water for about 10 minutes, until hard-boiled. Rinse them in iced water, shell and set aside to cool.

2. If necessary, remove the outer leaves from the chicory. Cut out the hard stalk in a cone shape and discard. Cut the chicory across into thin strips and put it into a strainer. Rinse and drain.

3. Coarsely chop the dill. Slice the eggs with an egg-slicer.

4. Mix together the mayonnaise, white wine vinegar and olive oil, season to taste with salt and pepper and stir in the sugar and curry powder. Mix in the dill.

5. Arrange the eggs and chicory on a plate and pour the sauce over them. Serve with wholemeal bread and butter.

Cream of pea soup with mint

If you want the soup to be particularly elegant and impressive, use strips of smoked salmon instead of diced ham.

Easy

Serves 2
1 small onion
15 g/1/2 oz butter
300 g/11 oz frozen peas
350 ml/12 fl oz chicken stock
2 thick slices of boiled ham, each
    about 50 g/2 oz
30 ml/2 tablespoons crème fraîche
    or double cream
5 ml/1 teaspoon lemon juice
1 sprig fresh mint
salt and freshly ground
    black pepper

Approximately per portion:
1,500 kJ/360 kcal
20 g protein, 22 g fat
19 g carbohydrate

● Approximate preparation
  time: 25 minutes

---

1. Finely dice the onion. Melt the butter in a heavy-based saucepan. Add the onion and sauté over a low heat, stirring occasionally, until soft and translucent.

2. Add the peas and pour in the chicken stock. Bring to the boil, reduce the heat, cover and simmer over a low heat for about 10 minutes.

3. Meanwhile, remove the fatty border from the ham and discard. Finely dice the meat.

4. Process the soup in a food processor or blender and return it to the saucepan. Alternatively, use the purée attachment of a hand-held electric mixer. Stir in the crème fraîche or cream and bring back to the boil. Season to taste with salt and pepper and stir in the lemon juice. Add the diced ham.

5. Cut the mint leaves into thin strips and sprinkle them over the pea soup. Serve immediately.

Above: Egg salad with chicory
Below: Cream of pea soup with mint

Chicken and vegetable stew

For a special occasion

Serves 2
*4 boneless, skinless chicken breasts,
  each about 90 g/3 1/2 oz
15 ml/1 tablespoon vegetable oil
1 small onion
1 large carrot
3 celery sticks
15 g/1 1/2 oz butter
120 ml/4 fl oz vegetable stock
45 ml/3 tablespoons white wine
30 ml/2 tablespoons crème fraîche
5 ml/1 teaspoon lemon juice
1/2 bunch fresh basil
salt and freshly ground pepper
rice, pasta or crusty bread, to serve*

Approximately per portion:
1,700 kJ/400 kcal
44 g protein, 21 g fat
7 g carbohydrate

● Approximate preparation
  time: 25 minutes

---

1. Cut the chicken breasts across
into 5 mm/1/4 inch thick slices.
Heat the oil in a heavy-based frying
pan. Add the chicken and fry over
a high heat, stirring frequently.
Remove the chicken from the pan,
season to taste with salt and
pepper and set aside.

2. Finely chop the onion. Coarsely
grate the carrot. Cut the celery
into thin strips.

3. Add the butter to the oil left in
the frying pan and heat until
melted. Add the vegetables and fry
over a low heat, stirring constantly.

4. Pour in the vegetable stock,
cover and braise for about
5 minutes.

5. Add the chicken and white wine
to the vegetables and bring to the
boil. Stir in the crème fraîche.
Season the stew to taste with salt
and pepper and stir in the lemon
juice. Tear the basil leaves into
strips and mix them into the stew.

6. Transfer the stew to warm
individual serving plates and serve
with rice, pasta or crusty bread.

Fried rice with prawns

Exclusive

Serves 2
*130 g/4 1/2 oz easy-cook rice
1 onion
2 garlic cloves
25 g/1 oz butter
150 g/5 oz frozen peas
120 ml/4 fl oz vegetable stock
200 g/7 oz peeled cooked prawns,
  thawed if frozen
30 ml/2 tablespoons soy sauce
lemon juice
salt and freshly ground white pepper*

Approximately per portion:
2,000 kJ/480 kcal
28 g protein, 16 g fat
62 g carbohydrate

● Approximate preparation
  time: 25 minutes

---

1. Cook the rice, according to the
instructions on the packet. Drain
thoroughly in a colander.

2. Meanwhile, finely chop the
onion. Melt the butter in a large
frying pan. Add the onion and
sauté, stirring occasionally, until soft
and translucent.

3. Crush the garlic and add it to
the pan, together with the peas.
Pour in the vegetable stock and
bring to the boil. Reduce the heat
to low, cover and simmer for
about 5 minutes.

4. Add the prawns and stir in the
rice. Season to taste with salt and
pepper, stir in the soy sauce and
lemon juice to taste and simmer
over a low heat for a further 3
minutes. Serve immediately.

Tip

If there is any of this dish left
over, allow it to cool and serve
it as a salad with an olive oil and
white wine vinegar dressing.

---

*Above: Chicken and vegetable stew
Below: Fried rice with prawns*

Chopped calf's liver in sherry sauce

Instead of calf's liver, you could substitute lamb's liver or chicken livers, but the flavour will not be so delicate.

Exquisite

Serves 2
1 small onion
115 g/4 oz oyster mushrooms
350 g/12 oz calf's liver, sliced
25 g/1 oz butter
4 potato cakes or croquettes
75 ml/5 tablespoons dry sherry
75 ml/5 tablespoons crème fraîche
lemon juice
salt and freshly ground white pepper
fresh parsley sprigs, to garnish
radicchio salad, to serve

Approximately per portion:
3,100 kJ/740 kcal
38 g protein, 45 g fat
40 g carbohydrate

● Approximate preparation
time: 25 minutes

---

1. Finely the onion. Cut the oyster mushrooms into thin strips. Cut the liver into thin strips.

2. Melt the butter in a frying pan. Add the liver and fry over a medium heat, stirring frequently, for 1–2 minutes, until cooked. Remove the liver from the pan, cover and set it aside.

3. Add the onion to the pan and sauté over a low heat, stirring

frequently, until soft and translucent. Add the mushrooms and fry them over a medium heat, stirring occasionally, until nearly all the liquid has evaporated.

4. Prepare the potato cakes or croquettes following the instructions on the packet.

5. Add the sherry to the mushrooms. Stir in the crème fraîche. Bring to the boil and season to taste with salt, pepper and lemon juice. Return the liver the pan and heat through gently, stirring to coat well with sauce.

6. Arrange the liver on two plates with the potato cakes and garnish with parsley sprigs. Serve with a radicchio salad.

Lamb and courgette stew

Easy

Serves 2
300 g/11 oz lamb fillet
30 ml/2 tablespoons olive oil
1 small onion
1 garlic clove
400 g/14 oz courgettes
250 ml/8 fl oz beef stock
5 ml/1 teaspoon dried thyme
5 ml/1 tablespoon lemon juice
salt and freshly ground black pepper

Approximately per portion:
1,300 kJ/310 kcal
35 g protein, 16 g fat
7 g carbohydrate

● Approximate preparation
time: 25 minutes

---

1. Dice the lamb. Heat the olive oil in a saucepan. Add the lamb and fry over a high heat, stirring frequently, for about 5 minutes, until well browned.

2. Finely chop the onion and garlic. Add them to the pan and fry over a low heat, stirring frequently, until soft and translucent.

3. Thinly slice the courgettes and add them to the pan. Fry, stirring constantly, for 1–2 minutes.

4. Pour in the stock and bring to the boil. Season to taste with salt and pepper and stir in the thyme and lemon juice. Cover and simmer over a low heat for about 10 minutes. Serve immediately.

Tip

If you do not like lamb, you can use meatballs made from frozen minced beef.

Above: Chopped calf's liver in sherry sauce
Below: Lamb and courgette stew

Sausages in vegetable broth

Bratwurst is a German smoked sausage made from very finely minced pork or veal and is pale in colour. Available from delicatessens, it should be eaten on the day of purchase.

Easy

Serves 2
2 carrots
2 onions
750 ml/1¼ pints water
1 bay leaf
3 black peppercorns
2.5 ml/½ teaspoon mustard seeds
75 ml/5 tablespoons red
    wine vinegar
12 Bratwurst sausages or other
    small smoked sausages, about
    400 g/14 oz
salt
4 slices rustic bread or ciabatta,
    to serve

1. Thinly slice the carrots. Thinly slice the onions and push them out into rings.

2. Bring the water to the boil in a large saucepan. Add a pinch of salt, the bay leaf, black peppercorns, mustard seeds, onion rings and sliced carrots and bring back to the boil. Lower the heat and simmer

for about 10 minutes. Add the red wine vinegar.

3. Add the sausages to the pan, cover and simmer over a low heat for 8–10 minutes. Do not allow the liquid to boil or the sausages will burst.

4. Serve the sausages in the broth with rustic bread or ciabatta.

Tip

Cook the vegetable broth in a covered pan for about 10 minutes in the microwave on HIGH. Add the sausages and cook for a further 3–5 minutes on MEDIUM.

Fried black pudding

This substantial and satisfying dish is particularly warming on chilly autumn and winter days and is quick and easy to make.

Economical

Serves 2
300 g/11 oz fresh or smoked
    black pudding
15 g/½ oz clarified butter
7.5 ml/1½ teaspoons chopped
    fresh marjoram or 2.5 ml/
    ½ teaspoon dried
1 small onion
1 tart apple
salt and freshly ground black pepper
Granary bread or chips,
    to serve

1. Skin the black pudding and cut it into 5 mm/¼ inch slices. Melt the clarified butter in a frying pan. Add the black pudding and fry on both sides over a medium heat. Season with salt and pepper and sprinkle the marjoram into the pan.

2. Thinly slice the onion. Add it to the pan and fry over a medium heat until it is soft and translucent.

3. Meanwhile, peel the apple, cut into quarters and core it. Cut the apple quarters across into thin slices. Add them to the pan and fry over a low heat for a further 5 minutes. Serve with Granary bread or chips.

Tip

Instead of black pudding, you can substitute 250 g/9 oz chicken livers.

Above: Fried black pudding
Below: Sausages in vegetable broth

Lamb's lettuce with croûtons

With plenty of good rustic bread, this salad makes a light supper for two. The quantities given are also sufficient to serve as a starter for four people.

Easy

Serves 2
4 slices streaky bacon, about
   115 g/4 oz
45–60 ml/3–4 tablespoons
   vegetable oil
2 slices bread
2 garlic cloves
5 ml/1 teaspoon strong mustard
45 ml/3 tablespoons red
   wine vinegar
115 g/4 oz lamb's lettuce
salt and freshly ground
   black pepper

Approximately per portion:
2,300 kJ/550 kcal
7 g protein, 54 g fat
12 g carbohydrate

● Approximate preparation
   time: 20 minutes

---

1. Remove the bacon rind, if necessary, and dice the bacon. Heat 5 ml/1 teaspoon of the oil in a heavy-based frying pan. Add the bacon and fry over a medium heat, stirring occasionally, until crisp. Remove it from the pan and drain on kitchen paper.

2. Remove the crusts from the bread and dice the slices. Add the bread cubes to the frying pan. Crush the garlic and add it to the pan. Fry the bread cubes, stirring frequently, until golden and crisp.

3. In a large bowl, mix together the mustard and vinegar and season to taste with salt and pepper. Add the remaining oil in a thin, continuous stream, whisking constantly with a balloon whisk. Continue whisking until the dressing becomes creamy.

4. Toss the lamb's lettuce and bacon in the dressing. Divide the salad between individual serving plates and sprinkle with the garlic-flavoured croûtons.

Spinach soup with salami

Economical

Serves 2
1 small onion
50 g/2 oz salami, thickly sliced
15 g/1/2 oz butter
150 g/5 oz frozen chopped spinach
350 ml/12 fl oz vegetable stock
pinch of freshly grated nutmeg
5 ml/1 teaspoon lemon juice
10 ml/2 teaspoons crème fraîche
salt and freshly ground black pepper

Approximately per portion:
1,200 kJ/290 kcal
8 g protein, 26 g fat
7 g carbohydrate

● Approximate preparation
   time: 20 minutes

---

1. Finely chop the onion. If necessary, skin the salami slices and then dice them finely.

2. Melt the butter in a saucepan. Add the diced salami and fry over a medium heat, stirring frequently. Remove it from the pan and set it aside.

3. Add the onion and sauté, stirring frequently, until it is soft and translucent. Add the spinach and pour in the vegetable stock. Bring to the boil over a low heat, cover and simmer for about 10 minutes.

4. Season the soup with salt and pepper to taste and stir in the nutmeg and lemon juice. Sprinkle in the diced salami. Divide the soup between warm individual soup plates and spoon a swirl of crème fraîche on top of each. Serve immediately.

Tip

This soup cooks even quicker in the microwave. Cook the soup on HIGH for about 4 minutes.

Above: Lamb's lettuce with croûtons
Below: Spinach soup with salami

Kohlrabi hotpot with smoked loin of pork

Easy

Serves 2
1 small onion
2 kohlrabi, about 600 g/1 lb 6 oz
15 g/¹/₂ oz butter
120 ml/4 fl oz chicken stock
75 ml/5 tablespoons double cream
300 g/11 oz smoked loin of pork
1 bunch of chives
pinch of freshly grated nutmeg
dash of Worcestershire sauce
salt and freshly ground white pepper
boiled potatoes or Granary bread,
*   to serve*

Approximately per portion:
2,500 kJ/600 kcal
38 g protein, 44 g fat
14 g carbohydrate

● Approximate preparation
time: 35 minutes

1. Finely chop the onion. Peel, quarter and thinly slice the kohlrabi.

2. Melt the butter in a saucepan. Add the onion and sauté over a low heat until soft and translucent. Add the kohlrabi and fry for 1–2 minutes. Pour in the stock and the cream. Bring to the boil, cover and simmer for about 15 minutes, until tender.

3. Meanwhile, finely dice the pork. Snip the chives.

Tip

You can cook the soup in the microwave in about 10 minutes on HIGH. Then add 75 ml/ 5 tablespoons chicken stock. It is even quicker if you use frozen kohlrabi.

4. Add the diced pork to the vegetables and heat through for about 3 minutes. Season to taste with salt and pepper and stir in the nutmeg and Worcestershire sauce. Mix in the chive rings. Serve immediately with boiled potatoes or Granary bread.

Haddock with cheese topping

Exquisite

Serves 2
30 ml/2 tablespoons breadcrumbs
15 ml/1 tablespoon olive oil
30 ml/2 tablespoons crème fraîche
50 g/2 oz grated Emmenthal cheese
1 lemon
3 garlic cloves
2 haddock fillets, each about
   150 g/5 oz, fresh or frozen
60 g/2½ oz easy-cook rice
1 bunch fresh dill
15 g/½ oz butter
vegetable oil, for brushing
salt and freshly ground black pepper
lemon wedges and fresh dill sprigs,
   to garnish

Approximately per portion:
2,600 kJ/620 kcal
42 g protein, 26 g fat
62 g carbohydrate

● Approximate preparation
  time: 25 minutes

Tip

You can cook the fish in a microwave on HIGH in about 5 minutes. Instead of haddock, you can use fresh or frozen cod.

1. Preheat the oven to 200°C/400°F/Gas 6. Mix together the breadcrumbs, olive oil, crème fraîche and cheese in a bowl.

2. Grate the lemon rind and squeeze out the juice. Add the lemon rind and 45 ml/3 tablespoons lemon juice to the cheese mixture. Crush the garlic and add it to the bowl. Mix thoroughly into a paste and season to taste with salt and pepper.

3. Brush a flat, ovenproof dish or roasting tin with oil. Season the fish fillets with salt and pepper and sprinkle them with a little lemon juice. Place them side by side in the prepared dish or tin. Spread the cheese mixture on the fish fillets and bake for 10–12 minutes.

4. Meanwhile, cook the rice following the instructions on the packet. Finely chop the dill and mix it into the rice, together with the butter. Transfer the fish and rice to individual warm plates, garnish with the lemon wedges and dill sprigs and serve immediately.

Pork goulash with sweetcorn

Easy

Serves 2
400 g/14 oz boneless pork shoulder
30 ml/2 tablespoons olive oil
1 small onion
2 garlic cloves
5 ml/1 teaspoon mild paprika
pinch of cayenne pepper
45 ml/3 tablespoons tomato purée
250 ml/8 fl oz chicken stock
200 g/7 oz can sweetcorn,
salt and freshly ground black pepper
snipped chives, to garnish
farfalle and mixed salad leaves,
*   to serve*

Approximately per portion:
2,600 kJ/620 kcal
41 g protein, 42 g fat
21 g carbohydrate

● Approximate preparation
   time: 45 minutes

---

1. Cut the pork into 2 cm/3/4 inch cubes. Heat the oil in a large saucepan. Add the pork and fry, stirring constantly, until it is lightly browned all over.

2. Thinly slice the onion and add it to the pan. Crush the garlic and add it to the pan.

3. Stir in the paprika and cayenne pepper and season to taste with salt and pepper. Stir in the tomato purée and cook, stirring constantly, for 1–2 minutes.

4. Add the stock, cover and simmer over a low heat for about

15 minutes. Drain the sweetcorn, add it to the pan and heat through for about 5 minutes.

5. Transfer to a warm individual plates. Garnish with snipped chives and serve with farfalle and mixed salad leaves.

Meat patties in caper and mustard sauce

Depending on your personal preferences, you can use minced beef, pork, lamb, chicken or even a mixture of different meats to make these patties.

Economical

Serves 2
50 g/2 oz day-old white bread
1 small onion
50 g/2 oz butter
300 g/11 oz mixed minced meat
1 egg
5 ml/1 teaspoon mild paprika
30 ml/2 tablespoons vegetable oil
1 small bottle of capers, drained
*   weight 20 g/3/4 oz*
5 ml/1 teaspoon medium mustard
120 ml /4 fl oz double cream
salt and freshly ground
*   black pepper*
mashed potatoes, garnished with
*   snipped chives, and tomato salad,*
*   to serve*

Approximately per portion:
3,500 kJ/830 kcal
34 g protein, 70 g fat
19 g carbohydrate

● Approximate preparation
   time: 30 minutes

---

1. Remove the crusts from the white bread and dice the slices. Place the diced bread in a small bowl. Add sufficient cold water to cover and set aside to soak.

2. Finely chop the onion. Heat half the butter in a small frying pan. Add half the diced onion and sauté, stirring frequently, until soft and translucent.

3. Drain the bread and squeeze out the excess water. Put the meat into a bowl, together with the bread. Add the cooked onion, the egg and paprika and season to taste with salt and pepper. Mix thoroughly. With damp hands form the mixture into 4 patties, pressing them fairly flat.

4. Heat the oil in a large frying pan. Add the patties and fry over a medium heat for about 7 minutes on each side.

5. Meanwhile, heat the remaining butter in a small pan. Add the remaining onion and sauté until soft and translucent. Stir in the capers, mustard and cream, bring to the boil and season to taste with salt and pepper.

6. Transfer the meat patties to two warm plates. Pour on the sauce and serve with mashed potatoes, garnished with snipped chives, and a tomato salad.

Above: Pork goulash with sweetcorn
Below: Meat patties in caper and mustard sauce

Venison medallions in cranberry sauce

Serve this festive meal on a special occasion – it would be a good choice for Christmas dinner.

Exclusive

Serves 2
1 small onion
15 g/¹/₂ oz butter
15 ml/1 tablespoon oil
8 venison medallions, each about 40 g/1¹/₂ oz
200 ml/7 fl oz red wine
2 juniper berries
1 bay leaf
1 clove
7.5 ml/1¹/₂ teaspoons fresh thyme or 2.5 ml/¹/₂ teaspoon dried
30 ml/2 tablespoons cranberries
15 ml/1 tablespoon tomato purée
120 ml/4 fl oz double cream
salt and freshly ground black pepper
potato croquettes and cranberry jelly (optional), to serve

Approximately per portion:
3,300 kJ/790 kcal
41 g protein, 39 g fat
49 g carbohydrate

● Approximate preparation time: 25 minutes

1. Finely chop the onion. Heat the butter and oil in a heavy-based frying pan until the butter has melted. Add the venison medallions and fry over a high heat for about 1–2 minutes on each side. Remove from the frying pan,

season to taste with salt and pepper, set aside and keep warm.

2. Add the onion to the pan and sauté until soft and translucent. Add the red wine. Crush the juniper berries and add them to the pan, together with the bay leaf, clove and thyme. Stir in the cranberries, bring to the boil and cook until reduced by about one third. Season to taste with salt and pepper.

3. Pour the sauce through a strainer, return it to the pan and stir in the tomato purée and double cream. Add the venison medallions, together with any cooking juices that may have run out. Warm them through in the sauce for about 3 minutes.

4. Arrange the venison medallions on two warm plates and pour on the cranberry cream. Serve with potato croquettes and cranberry jelly, if desired.

Calf's kidneys in chervil sauce

Exquisite

Serves 2
115 g/4 oz fresh chervil
250 g/9 oz calf's kidneys
25 g/1 oz butter
2 garlic cloves
75 ml/5 tablespoons dry white wine
60 ml/4 tablespoons crème fraîche
pinch of cayenne pepper
5 ml/1 teaspoon lemon juice
salt and freshly ground white pepper
fresh sprigs of chervil, to garnish
potato pancakes or fried bread, to serve

Approximately per portion:
2,300 kJ/550 kcal
23 g protein, 37 g fat
25 g carbohydrate

● Approximate preparation time: 20 minutes

1. Finely chop the chervil and set aside until required.

2. Remove the membrane from the kidneys and cut them into 5 mm/¹/₄ inch slices. Melt the butter in a frying pan. Add the kidneys and fry over a medium heat for about 1 minute on each side. Season to taste with salt and pepper and remove from the pan.

3. Crush the garlic and add it to the frying pan. Fry over a low heat until soft. Stir in the white wine and crème fraîche. Season to taste with salt and pepper and stir in the cayenne pepper and lemon juice. Simmer over a low heat for about 2 minutes.

4. Return the kidneys to the pan and heat through, but do not overcook. Just before serving sprinkle the chervil over them.

5. Serve the kidneys immediately, garnished with chervil sprigs and with potato pancakes or fried bread.

Above: Venison medallions in cranberry sauce
Below: Calf's kidneys in chervil sauce

Warm vegetable salad with roast beef

Exquisite

Serves 2
2 large carrots, about 200 g/7 oz
1 courgette, about 200 g/7 oz
30 ml/2 tablespoons olive oil
115 g/4 oz roast beef,
    thinly sliced
juice of ½ lemon
1 bunch of basil
salt and freshly ground black pepper

Approximately per portion:
932 kJ/221 kcal
13 g protein, 16 g fat
7 g carbohydrate

● Approximate preparation
   time: 20 minutes

---

1. Thinly slice the carrots and courgette.

2. Heat the oil in a frying pan. Add the vegetables and fry over a low heat, stirring frequently, for about 5 minutes, until they are tender, but still firm to the bite.

3. Using a sharp knife, cut the roast beef into thin strips.

4. Put the vegetables into a bowl, together with the oil and the roast beef strips.

5. Sprinkle in the lemon juice and season to taste with salt and pepper. Add the basil leaves and mix thoroughly. Serve while the salad is still warm.

Pork with beansprouts

This is a quick and easy, if slightly 'cheating', version of a classic Chinese dish.

Exquisite

Serves 2
400 g/14 oz pork fillet
5 ml/1 teaspoon cornflour
25 g/1 oz clarified butter
3 garlic cloves
200 g/7 oz fresh beansprouts or
    175 g/6 oz canned beansprouts
120 ml/4 fl oz chicken stock
1 bunch fresh flat leaf parsley
30 ml/2 tablespoons soy sauce
salt and freshly ground black pepper
cellophane noodles or rice, to serve

Approximately per portion:
2,300 kJ/530 kcal
43 g protein, 40 g fat
6 g carbohydrate

● Approximate preparation
   time: 20 minutes

---

1. Cut the pork across the grain into thin strips. Sprinkle it with the cornflour and then rub it well into the meat.

2. Heat the clarified butter in a large frying pan. Add the pork and fry over a high heat, stirring constantly, until browned all over. Season to taste with salt and pepper. Remove from the pan, cover and set it aside.

3. Crush the garlic and add it to the frying pan. Fry over a low heat until soft.

4. Rinse the fresh beansprouts and pick over, if using. Drain and rinse the canned beansprouts, if using. Add the beansprouts to the frying pan and fry for about 5 minutes.

5. Pour in the stock.. Finely chop the parsley and add to the pan.

6. Stir in the soy sauce and bring to the boil. Return the pork to the pan and warm through. Serve with cellophane noodles or rice.

Tip

Light soy sauce has more flavour than the sweeter, dark soy sauce.

Above: Pork with beansprouts
Below: Warm vegetable salad with roast beef

Turkey curry with banana and coconut rice

Exquisite

Serves 2
1 small onion
2 turkey escalopes, each about
   175 g/6 oz
1 banana
130 g/4$^{1}/_{2}$ oz easy-cook rice
15 g/1$^{1}/_{2}$ oz clarified butter
15 ml/1 tablespoon curry powder
45 ml/3 tablespoons crème fraîche
5 ml/1 teaspoon lemon juice
30 ml/2 tablespoons desiccated
   coconut
salt and freshly ground black pepper

Approximately per portion:
2,900 kJ/690 kcal
43 g protein, 28 g fat
74 g carbohydrate

● Approximate preparation
  time: 25 minutes

---

1. Finely chop the onion. Cut the turkey into strips about 1 cm/$^{1}/_{2}$ inch wide. Peel the banana and cut into thick slices.

2. Bring a large saucepan of well-salted water to the boil. Cook the rice until tender, following the packet instructions. Tip into a colander and drain well.

3. Heat the clarified butter in a large heavy-based frying pan. Add the turkey and fry over a medium heat, stirring frequently, until golden all over. Add the onions and fry until soft and translucent.

4. Add the banana slices to the pan and fry for 1–2 minutes. Sprinkle the curry powder over them and cook until lightly browned. Season to taste with salt and pepper. Add the crème fraîche and stir in the lemon juice.

5. Dry-fry the coconut in a non-stick pan, stirring constantly, until light brown.

6. Mix the banana slices and coconut with the drained rice and then arrange the rice on two warm plates with the turkey curry. Serve immediately.

Veal with mushrooms

If preferred, you can make this dish with pork fillet.

Easy

Serves 2
2 veal escalopes, each about
   175 g/6 oz
15 g/1$^{1}/_{2}$ oz clarified butter
150 g/5 oz button mushrooms
45 ml/3 tablespoons dry
   white wine
120 ml/4 fl oz crème fraîche or
   soured cream
115 g/4 oz fresh chervil
salt and freshly ground white pepper
ribbon pasta, to serve

Approximately per portion:
2,100 kJ/500 kcal
41 g protein, 36 g fat
3 g carbohydrate

● Approximate preparation
  time: 30 minutes

---

1. Cut the veal escalopes in half lengthways, then cut across into narrow strips.

2. Melt the clarified butter in a frying pan. Add the veal and fry, stirring frequently, until browned on all sides. Remove it from the pan, season to taste with salt and pepper, cover and set aside.

3. Add the mushrooms to the pan and fry over a medium heat, stirring constantly, until nearly all the liquid has evaporated.

4. Add the wine, bring to the boil and cook until reduced. Stir in the crème fraîche or soured cream and bring the mixture back to the boil. Return the veal to the pan and heat for about 2 minutes until piping hot. Season to taste with salt and pepper.

5. Sprinkle the chervil leaves over the veal, transfer to a warm serving dish and serve immediately with ribbon pasta.

Tip

You can make this delicious veal dish even more special by using wild mushrooms, such as ceps, chanterelles or oyster mushrooms. A less expensive, but still tasty alternative would be to use a mixture of wild and cultivated varieties.

Above: Turkey curry with banana and coconut rice
Below: Veal with mushrooms

Prawns and melon salad

This would make a delicious light lunch or *al fresco* summer supper. The quantities are sufficient to serve four as a first course.

Exquisite

Serves 2
I small iceberg lettuce
I small ripe melon
115 g/4 oz peeled, cooked prawns, thawed if frozen
I bunch fresh basil
juice of I lemon
pinch of cayenne pepper
45 ml/3 tablespoons olive oil
salt and freshly ground black pepper
French bread, to serve

Approximately per portion:
1,000 kJ/ 240 kcal
13 g protein, 13 g fat
17 g carbohydrate ·

● Approximate preparation time: 25 minutes

I. Separate the lettuce leaves. Cut the melon in half across and scoop out the seeds with a spoon. Either remove the flesh with a melon-baller or cut the melon into wedges, cut out the flesh and dice it.

2. Put the prawns in a serving bowl, together with the lettuce and melon. Scatter the basil leaves on top.

3. Mix together the lemon juice, cayenne pepper and olive oil and season to taste with salt and pepper. Pour the dressing over the salad and toss thoroughly to mix. Serve with French bread.

Fillet steaks in orange sauce

Fillet steak is very expensive, but it is incomparably tender. No other type of steak really makes an adequate substitute.
For a special occasion

Serves 2
130 g/4¹/2 oz easy-cook rice
25 g/I oz butter
2 beef fillet steaks, each about 175 g/6 oz
I orange, about 200 g/7 oz
45 ml/3 tablespoons beef stock
15 ml/I tablespoon balsamic vinegar
30 ml/2 tablespoons chopped pistachio nuts
salt and freshly ground white pepper

Approximately per portion:
2,300 kJ/550 kcal
36 g protein, 25 g fat
53 g carbohydrate

● Approximate preparation time: 15 minutes

I. Cook the rice in salted boiling water, following the packet instructions. Drain thoroughly.

2. Meanwhile, melt half the butter in a frying pan. Add the steaks and fry for about I minute on each side. Remove from the pan and season to taste with salt and pepper. Cover and set aside.

3. Cut the orange in half, cut off two slices and set aside for the garnish. Squeeze the orange halves. Pour the orange juice into the frying pan. Add the stock and vinegar and simmer, uncovered, over a low heat for about 2 minutes. Season to taste with salt and pepper.

4. Return the steaks to the pan and heat through in the sauce for about 2 minutes.

5. Melt the remaining butter in another pan, toss the rice in it and mix in the pistachio nuts.

6. Arrange the steaks on warm individual serving plates. Pour on the orange sauce and garnish with the reserved orange slices. Serve immediately with the pistachio rice.

Tip

Balsamic vinegar, which is made only in the area around Modena in northern Italy, has a unique, mellow, sweet-and-sour flavour. It is made from grape juices concentrated over a low heat and then fermented in a succession of wooden barrels. It is expensive, but a little goes a long way.

Above: Prawns and melon salad
Below: Fillet steaks in orange sauce

Prawns in saffron cream

Exclusive

Serves 2
50 g/2 oz button or chestnut
mushrooms
25 g/1 oz butter
2.5 ml/^{1}/$_2$ teaspoon saffron strands
200 ml/7 fl oz double cream
150 g/5 oz dried fettuccine
5 ml/1 teaspoon lemon juice
250 g/9 oz peeled cooked prawns,
thawed if frozen
salt and freshly ground white pepper
mixed salad leaves, to serve

Approximately per portion:
3,400 kJ/810 kcal
35 g protein, 50 g fat
54 g carbohydrate

● Approximate preparation
time: 30 minutes

---

1. Cut the mushrooms into quarters. Melt the butter in a heavy-based frying pan and fry the mushrooms over a medium heat, stirring frequently.

2. Stir in the saffron strands. Pour in the cream and simmer the sauce, uncovered, until it has reduced by half.

3. Meanwhile, bring a large saucepan of well-salted water to the boil. Add the fettuccine, bring back to the boil and cook for 8–10 minutes, until the pasta is tender, but still firm to the bite.

4. Season the saffron cream to taste with salt and pepper and stir in the lemon juice.

5. Add the prawns and heat through in the sauce for about 3 minutes. Transfer the prawns and sauce to individual warm plates, together with the pasta. Serve with mixed salad leaves.

Tip

The black vein that runs along the length of a prawn is not poisonous, but can spoil the flavour. It is best to remove it with the point of a sharp knife before cooking.

Poached salmon with cress sauce

Exquisite

Serves 2
2 salmon cutlets, each about
200 g/7 oz
15 ml/1 tablespoon lemon juice
1 small onion
25 g/1 oz butter
105 ml/7 tablespoons dry
white wine
120 ml/4 fl oz crème fraîche or
sour cream
1 punnet of cress
salt and freshly ground white pepper
rice and green salad, to serve

Approximately per portion:
3,500 kJ/850 kcal
42 g protein, 65 g fat
7 g carbohydrate

● Approximate preparation
time: 20 minutes

---

1. Rinse the salmon under cold running water and pat dry with kitchen paper. Sprinkle each cutlet with about 5 ml/1 teaspoon lemon juice and season to taste with salt.

2. Finely chop the onion. Melt the butter in a frying pan. Add the onion and sauté over a low heat until it is soft and translucent.

3. Add the salmon and fry it on both sides. Pour in the wine and simmer over a low heat for about 5 minutes. Remove from the pan, cover and set aside.

4. Stir the crème fraîche or soured cream into the pan, bring to the boil and cook until reduced by one third. Season to taste with salt and pepper and stir in the remaining lemon juice. Return the salmon to the pan and heat through.

5. Snip the cress directly into the frying pan.

6. Arrange the salmon cutlets on individual warm plates and pour the sauce over them. Serve with rice and a green salad.

Above: Prawns in saffron cream
Below: Poached salmon with cress sauce

VEGETARIAN TREATS

Chinese vegetable rice

Exotic

Serves 2
1 garlic clove
1 cm/$^1/_2$ inch piece of fresh
    root ginger
25 g/1 oz butter
300 g/11 oz mixed Chinese
    vegetables, fresh or frozen
130 g/4$^1/_2$ oz easy-cook rice
60 ml/4 tablespoons dark soy sauce
60 ml/4 tablespoons Chinese rice
    wine or dry sherry
2.5 ml/$^1/_2$ teaspoon Chinese five
    spice powder
salt and freshly ground pepper

Approximately per portion:
2,200 kJ/520 kcal
10 g protein, 25 g fat
68 g carbohydrate

● Approximate preparation
   time: 20 minutes

---

1. Finely chop the garlic and ginger. Melt the butter in a large frying pan. Add the garlic and ginger and stir-fry over a medium heat for 1–2 minutes.

2. Add the mixed Chinese vegetables and stir-fry for 3 minutes or according to the packet instructions, until they are tender, but still firm to the bite.

3. Cook the rice in a large saucepan of boiling salted water, following the packet instructions.

4. Add the soy sauce and the rice wine or sherry to the frying pan.

Season to taste with salt and pepper and stir in the Chinese five spice powder. Gently mix the rice with the vegetables and transfer to a warm serving dish and serve immediately.

Tip

This vegetable rice can also be served as an accompaniment to prawns or fish.

Broccoli with cheese topping and sesame seeds

Instead of broccoli, you could use cauliflower or green asparagus.
Economical

Serves 2
300 g/11 oz broccoli, fresh
    or frozen
15 ml/1 tablespoon lemon juice
30 ml/2 tablespoons sesame seeds
pinch of freshly grated nutmeg
200 g/7 oz Gorgonzola cheese
2 eggs
butter, for greasing
salt and freshly ground black pepper
mashed potatoes, to serve

Approximately per portion:
2,500 kJ/600 kcal
33 g protein, 47 g fat
5 g carbohydrate

● Approximate preparation
   time: 25 minutes

---

1. Divide fresh broccoli, if using, into individual florets. Bring a large saucepan of well-salted water to the boil and add the lemon juice. Add the broccoli and cook for about 3 minutes. Drain, rinse in iced water and drain well again.

2. Dry-fry the sesame seeds in a non-stick pan until they are golden brown and giving off their aroma. Preheat the oven to 200°C/400°F/Gas 6.

3. Grease an ovenproof dish with butter. Put the broccoli into the prepared dish and season to taste with salt, pepper and nutmeg. Sprinkle the sesame seeds over the broccoli florets.

4. Crumble the Gorgonzola into a bowl, add the eggs and beat to a smooth mixture with a hand-held electric mixer.

5. Pour the cheese mixture over the broccoli. Bake in the oven for about 15 minutes. Serve immediately straight from the dish with mashed potatoes.

Tip

Bake this dish golden brown in the microwave for about 6 minutes on HIGH.

Above: Chinese vegetable rice
Below: Broccoli with cheese topping and sesame seeds

Stuffed tomatoes

These tomatoes may be served immediately or allowed to cool slightly and then served, Greek style, when tepid.

Economical

Serves 2
4 large beefsteak tomatoes
1 bunch fresh basil
4 garlic cloves
75 ml/5 tablespoons breadcrumbs
45 ml/3 tablespoons olive oil, plus
  extra for brushing
50 g/2 oz grated Emmenthal or
  Gouda cheese
salt and freshly ground black pepper

Approximately per portion:
2,100 kJ/500 kcal
15 g protein, 33 g fat
32 g carbohydrate

● Approximate preparation
  time: 30 minutes

Tip

Bake the stuffed tomatoes in the microwave for 6–8 minutes on MEDIUM. Serve the tomatoes with French bread. To make them crispy, you can cook them in the oven for the last 10 minutes.

1. Cut a thin slice from the round end of each tomato. Scoop out the flesh and seeds. Discard the seeds and coarsely chop the tomato flesh. Sprinkle the inside of the tomatoes with salt and pepper to taste. Preheat the oven to 220°C/425°F/Gas 7.

2. Reserve 2 sprigs for the garnish, roughly tear up the remaining basil leaves and put them into a bowl. Crush the garlic and add it to the bowl. Add the breadcrumbs, olive oil and tomato flesh and mix thoroughly.

3. Divide the mixture between the tomato shells. Brush an ovenproof dish just large enough to hold the tomatoes with olive oil. Put the tomatoes into the dish and sprinkle them with the cheese.

4. Bake the stuffed tomatoes in the oven for 15–20 minutes, until the filling is golden brown. Serve hot or warm, garnished with the reserved basil sprigs.

Poached eggs on creamed leeks

Easy

Serves 2
450 g/1 lb frozen leeks
butter, for greasing
60 ml/4 tablespoons vinegar
75 g/3 oz grated Emmenthal or
*   Gouda cheese*
120 ml/4 fl oz double cream
freshly grated nutmeg
salt and freshly ground black pepper
fresh parsley sprigs, to garnish
boiled potatoes, to serve

Approximately per portion:

2,800 kJ/670 kcal

31 g protein, 52 g fat

19 g carbohydrate

● Approximate preparation
  time: 25 minutes

Tip

Thaw the leeks in the
microwave following the packet
instructions. Put the poached
eggs on top, spread with the
cheese mixture and bake for
about 6 minutes on HIGH.
Instead of leeks you can use
frozen spinach.

1. Cook the leeks following the
instructions on the packet. Grease
an ovenproof dish with butter and
put the leeks into it. Preheat the
oven to 180°C/350°F/Gas 4.

2. Bring about 1 litre/1³/₄ pints
water to the boil. Add a pinch of
salt and the vinegar. Break the eggs
singly into a cup and slip each
carefully into the water. Poach
them over a low heat for about
3 minutes. Remove with a slotted
spoon, drain and arrange them on
top of the leeks.

3. Mix together the cheese and
cream and season to taste with
salt, pepper and nutmeg. Spread
the cheese mixture over the eggs.

4. Bake in the oven for about
10 minutes, until the cheese has
melted and the top is golden
brown. Garnish with parsley
sprigs and serve immediately with
boiled potatoes.

Cream of artichoke soup

The delicate flavour of artichoke hearts is ideal for preparing a rich, creamy soup.

Exclusive

Serves 2
1 onion
25 g/1 oz butter
250 g/9 oz drained, canned artichoke hearts,
475 ml/16 fl oz vegetable stock
30 ml/2 tablespoons crème fraîche
lemon juice
Worcestershire sauce
1/2 bunch fresh flat leaf parsley
salt and freshly ground white pepper

Approximately per portion:
1,100 kJ/260 kcal
5 g protein, 22 g fat
15 g carbohydrate

● Approximate preparation time: 25 minutes

---

1. Finely chop the onion. Melt the butter in a saucepan. Add the onion and sauté over a low heat, stirring frequently, until it is soft and translucent.

2. Cut the artichoke hearts into quarters. Add them to the pan and sauté, stirring occasionally, for 1–2 minutes. Pour in the vegetable stock, bring to the boil, cover and simmer for about 10 minutes. Finely chop the parsley.

3. Purée the soup with the purée attachment of a hand-held electric mixer or process in a food processor and return to the pan. Add the crème fraîche. Bring to the boil and season to taste with salt, pepper, lemon juice and Worcestershire sauce. Sprinkle with the chopped parsley and serve immediately.

Mushrooms with dumplings

This recipe is particularly delicious made with wild mushrooms. You could also use button, chestnut or mixed mushrooms.

Easy

Serves 2
500 g/1 1/4 lb oyster mushrooms
1 onion
2 garlic cloves
25 g/1 oz butter
5 ml/1 teaspoon dried thyme
30 ml/2 tablespoon tomato purée
120 ml/4 fl oz crème fraîche
250 ml/8 fl oz vegetable stock
4 ready-made dumplings
1 bunch of fresh flat leaf parsley
5 ml/1 teaspoon lemon juice
salt and freshly ground black pepper

Approximately per portion:
2,700 kJ/640 kcal
14 g protein, 40 g fat
44 g carbohydrate

● Approximate preparation time: 30 minutes

---

1. Cut or tear the mushrooms into 2 cm/3/4 inch long strips. Finely chop the onion. Melt the butter in a large frying pan. Add the onion and sauté over a low heat until soft and translucent. Crush the garlic and add it to the frying pan.

2. Add the mushrooms to the pan and fry, stirring occasionally, for about 10 minutes. Season to taste with salt and pepper and add the thyme. Stir in the tomato purée. Add the crème fraîche and the vegetable stock and simmer for a further 5 minutes.

3. Cook the dumplings following the packet instructions.

4. Finely chop the parsley. Stir the lemon juice into the mushroom mixture and sprinkle the parsley over it.

5. Put the dumplings on two deep plates, spoon the mushroom mixture next to them and serve.

Above: Cream of artichoke soup
Below: Mushrooms with dumplings

Fried vegetables with feta cheese

Easy

Serves 2
1 large red pepper, about
   150 g/5 oz
2 small courgettes, about
   250 g/9 oz
1 small onion
30 ml/2 tablespoons olive oil
30 ml/2 tablespoons tomato purée
105 ml/7 tablespoons vegetable
   stock
5 ml/1 teaspoon fresh Italian
   mixed herbs
115 g/4 oz feta cheese
salt and freshly ground black pepper
French bread, to serve

Approximately per portion:
1,100 kJ/260 kcal
11 g protein, 20 g fat
9 g carbohydrate

● Approximate preparation
   time: 20 minutes

1. Core and seed the pepper and cut it into quarters, then into thin strips. Thinly slice the courgettes. Thinly slice the onion and push it out into rings.

2. Heat the olive oil in a saucepan. Add the onion rings and sauté over a low heat until soft and translucent. Add the pepper and the courgettes and fry, stirring constantly, for about 3 minutes.

3. Stir in the tomato purée and vegetable stock. Season to taste with salt and pepper and add the

mixed herbs. Reduce the heat, cover and simmer for about 8 minutes.

4. Crumble the cheese, mix it into the vegetables and heat through. Serve immediately with crusty French bread.

Tip

Feta is a white crumbly cheese that is traditionally made from ewe's milk, although nowadays it is more often made from cow's milk. It is preserved in brine, which, if it is left for a long time, tends to make the cheese hard and sour. In Greece, feta is eaten or cooked when very fresh. For export, it is usually vacuum packed. Many other countries besides Greece now produce feta.

Cucumber soup with smoked salmon

Exclusive

Serves 2
1 cucumber, about 600 g/
   1 lb 6 oz
1 shallot
15 g/1 1/2 oz butter
475 ml/16 fl oz vegetable stock
pinch of cayenne pepper
pinch of ground coriander
50 g/2 oz smoked salmon
30 ml/2 tablespoons crème fraîche
salt
fresh dill sprigs, to garnish

Approximately per portion:
980 kJ/230 kcal
9 g protein, 18 g fat
8 g carbohydrate

● Approximate preparation
   time: 20 minutes

1. Peel the cucumber, and cut it into quarters lengthways. Remove the seeds and cut the flesh into thin slices.

2. Finely chop the shallot. Melt the butter in a saucepan. Add the shallot and cucumber and sauté over a low heat.

3. Pour in the vegetable stock, season to taste with salt and stir in the cayenne pepper and ground coriander. Cover and simmer over a medium heat for about 10 minutes.

4. Meanwhile, cut the smoked salmon into strips.

5. Purée the soup with the purée attachment of a hand-held electric mixer or process in a food processor and return the purée to the pan. Stir in the crème fraîche, bring to the boil and season to taste with salt.

6. Add the salmon to the soup. Pour the soup into individual warm bowls, garnish with the dill and serve immediately.

Above: Fried vegetables with feta cheese
Below: Cucumber soup with smoked salmon

Lentil soup with Kabanos sausage

Instead of lentils, you can use kidney or haricot beans and instead of the sausage, you can use bacon or smoked fish.

Economical

Serves 2
1 Kabanos sausage or other smoked spicy sausage, about 115 g/4 oz
15 ml/1 tablespoon vegetable oil
1 small onion
45 ml/3 tablespoons tomato purée
250 ml/8 fl oz beef stock
400 g/14 oz can lentils,
pinch of medium paprika
5 ml/1 teaspoon red wine vinegar
salt and freshly ground black pepper
crusty bread, to serve

```
Approximately per portion:
2,800 kJ/670 kcal
39 g protein, 24 g fat
72 g carbohydrate
● Approximate preparation
  time: 15 minutes
```

1. Slice the sausage. Heat the oil in a saucepan. Add the sausage slices and fry over a medium heat until they are crisp. Remove from the pan and set aside.

2. Finely chop the onion. Add it to the pan and sauté over a medium heat until soft and translucent. Stir in the tomato purée. Pour in the stock, add the lentils and simmer for about 10 minutes.

3. Season to taste with salt and pepper and stir in the paprika and red wine vinegar. Return the sausage slices to the pan and heat through. Serve immediately with crusty bread.

Macaroni cheese

This is a tasty variation on a cheap and cheerful, highly popular supper dish. You can vary the cheese according to taste.

Easy

Serves 2
250 g/9 oz dried elbow macaroni
2 onions
25 g/1 oz butter, plus extra for greasing
150 g/5 oz grated Cheddar cheese
salt and freshly ground black pepper
crisp green salad and chive vinaigrette, to serve

```
Approximately per portion:
3,600 kJ/860 kcal
39 g protein, 39 g fat
88 g carbohydrate
● Approximate preparation
  time: 25 minutes
```

1. Bring a large saucepan of well-salted water to the boil. Add the macaroni, bring back to the boil and cook for 8–10 minutes, until tender but still firm to the bite. Drain, rinse in hot water and drain again. Preheat the oven to 220°C/425°F/ Gas 7.

2. Thinly slice the onions and push the slices out into rings. Melt the butter in a frying pan. Add the

onions and fry, stirring constantly, until golden brown.

3. Grease an ovenproof dish with butter. Put in the macaroni and onion rings in layers, sprinkling each layer with grated cheese and seasoning with salt and pepper. Finish with a layer of cheese.

4. Bake in the oven for about 10 minutes, until the cheese has melted. Serve with a crisp green salad and a chive vinaigrette.

Tip

You can cook the macaroni cheese in the microwave for 6–8 minutes on HIGH, until the cheese has melted.

Above: Lentil soup with Kabanos sausage
Below: Macaroni cheese

Rigatoni with herb sauce

You can use any shape of hollow pasta for this recipe, such as penne, pipe rigati or even macaroni.

Easy

Serves 2
15 g/$1^1/_2$ oz butter
3–4 garlic cloves
120 ml/4 fl oz double cream
200 g/7 oz herb cream cheese
5 ml/1 teaspoon dried oregano
5 ml/1 teaspoon dried thyme
250 g/9 oz dried rigatoni
50 g/2 oz Parmesan cheese, freshly grated
salt and freshly ground black pepper

Approximately per portion:
5,200 kJ/1200 kcal
40 g protein, 80 g fat
90 g carbohydrate

- Approximate preparation time: 25 minutes

---

1. Melt the butter in a frying pan. Crush the garlic, add it to the pan and fry over a low heat, stirring constantly, for 1–2 minutes.

2. Pour in the cream. Add the cream cheese and stir until the cream cheese has completely melted. Season to taste with salt and pepper, stir in the oregano and thyme, and keep the sauce warm over a very low heat.

3. Meanwhile, bring a large saucepan of well-salted water to the boil. Add the rigatoni, bring back to the boil and cook for 10–12 minutes, until it is tender, but still firm to the bite. Drain well.

4. Mix the pasta with the sauce in a serving bowl, using 2 large forks, sprinkle with the Parmesan and serve immediately.

Baked pasta with corned beef

Economical

Serves 2
150 g/5 oz dried tagliatelle
150 g/5 oz peas, frozen or canned
200 g/7 oz can corned beef
200 ml/7 fl oz double cream
2 eggs
50 g/2 oz grated Cheddar cheese
pinch of hot paprika
butter, for greasing
salt and freshly ground pepper

Approximately per portion:
4,000 kJ/950 kcal
41 g protein, 61 g fat
62 g carbohydrate

- Approximate preparation time: 25 minutes

---

1. Bring a large saucepan of well-salted water to the boil. Add the tagliatelle, bring back to the boil and cook for about 8 minutes, until it is tender, but still firm to the bite. Drain thoroughly and rinse in boiling water so that it does not stick together.

2. Preheat the oven to 200°C/400°F/Gas 6. Thaw frozen peas a little, if using. Thoroughly drain canned peas, if using.

3. First cut the corned beef into thin slices, then into thin strips. Mix it with the pasta, together with the peas. Grease an ovenproof dish with butter and put the pasta mixture into it.

4. Mix together the cream, eggs and cheese. Season to taste with salt and pepper and stir in the paprika. Pour the cheese mixture over the pasta.

5. Bake the pasta in the oven for 15–20 minutes, until the top is golden and bubbling. Serve immediately straight from the dish.

Tip

You can bake the pasta in the microwave for 5–7 minutes on HIGH.

Above: Baked pasta with corned beef
Below: Rigatoni with herb sauce

Salami pizza with olives

Easy

Serves 2
ready-made pizza base, about
   250 g/9 oz
250 g/9 oz canned chopped
   tomatoes
5 ml/1 teaspoon dried rosemary
5 ml/1 teaspoon dried oregano
5 ml/1 teaspoon dried thyme
115 g/4 oz salami, sliced
30 ml/2 tablespoons green
   olives, stoned
130 g/4^1/2 oz mozzarella cheese
15 ml/1 tablespoon olive oil
salt and freshly ground black pepper

Approximately per portion:
3,400 kJ/810 kcal
32 g protein, 50 g fat
58 g carbohydrate

● Approximate preparation
   time: 35 minutes

---

1. Preheat the oven to 200°C/
400°F/Gas 6. Line a baking sheet
with baking paper and place the
pizza base on it.

2. Spoon the tomatoes on to the
base, spreading them evenly.
Season to taste with salt and
pepper and sprinkle with the
rosemary, thyme and oregano.
Arrange the salami slices on top
and dot with the olives.

3. Cut the mozzarella into 5
mm/^{1}/4 inch slices and place these
on the pizza. Finally, sprinkle the
pizza with the olive oil and season
with salt and pepper again.

4. Bake the pizza in the middle of
the oven for about 20 minutes,
until hot and bubbling. Cut in slices
and serve immediately.

Scrambled eggs on toast with prawns and dill

The trick to making perfect
scrambled egg is to avoid
overcooking. Otherwise, it will dry
and out and become rubbery.

Easy

Serves 2
1 small onion
1 bunch of fresh dill
4 eggs
30 ml/2 tablespoons crème fraîche
pinch of freshly grated nutmeg
200 g/7 oz peeled, cooked prawns,
   thawed if frozen
25 g/1 oz butter mixed with
   5 ml/1 teaspoon chopped fresh
   herbs, such as parsley or dill
2 slices Granary or rustic bread
salt and freshly ground
   white pepper

Approximately per portion:
2,236 kJ/534 kcal
36 g protein, 32 g fat
26 g carbohydrate

● Approximate preparation
   time: 25 minutes

---

1. Finely chop the onion. Chop the
fresh dill.

2. In a bowl, beat the eggs with
the crème fraîche. Season to taste
with salt and pepper and stir in the

nutmeg. Stir in two thirds of the
dill and the prawns.

3. Melt half the herb butter in a
frying pan. Add the onion and
sauté over a low heat for about
3 minutes.

4. Add the egg mixture and cook
over a low heat, stirring frequently,
for about 8 minutes, until set.

5. Meanwhile, toast the bread and
spread it with the remaining herb
butter. Divide the scrambled egg
mixture between the slices of
toast, sprinkle with the remaining
dill and serve immediately.

Tip

Instead of prawns, you can mix
the eggs with tuna, ham,
spinach, diced tomatoes or just
chopped fresh herbs. Serve
with a mixed salad.

Above: Salami pizza with olives
Below: Scrambled eggs on toast with
prawns and dill

Baked red cabbage with liver sausage

Easy

Serves 2
2 portions of instant mashed potato
butter, for greasing
500 g/1 1/4 lb can red cabbage
250 g/9 oz coarse liver sausage
75 g/3 oz grated Cheddar cheese
pinch of freshly grated nutmeg
salt and freshly ground black pepper

Approximately per portion:
3,900 kJ/930 kcal
33 g protein, 68 g fat
46 g carbohydrate

● Approximate preparation
time: 25 minutes

---

1. Make the mashed potato, following the packet instructions.

2. Preheat the oven to 240°C/ 475°F/Gas 9. Grease an ovenproof dish. Put half the cabbage into it.

3. Finely chop the liver sausage and spread it on top of the cabbage. Then cover evenly with the remaining cabbage.

4. Mix the cheese with the mashed potato. Season to taste with salt and pepper and stir in the nutmeg. Spread the potato on top of the red cabbage and smooth the surface.

5. Bake in the oven for about 10 minutes, then reduce the oven temperature to 200°C/400°F/

Gas 6. Continue to bake for a further 10 minutes, until the top is golden brown. Serve hot.

Tip

Instead of red cabbage, you can use sauerkraut.

Baked steaklets

These spicy steaklets also make a good starter for four people.

Easy

Serves 2
30 ml/2 tablespoons vegetable oil
4 frozen steaklets, about
*   300 g/11 oz*
1 garlic clove
1 tomato
130 g/4 1/2 oz mozzarella cheese
salt and freshly ground
*   black pepper*
2 fresh basil sprigs, to garnish
mixed salad and rustic bread,
*   to serve*

Approximately per portion:
2,500 kJ/600 kcal
35 g protein, 42 g fat
19 g carbohydrate

● Approximate preparation
time: 15 minutes

---

1. Heat the oil in a frying pan. Add the steaklets, without thawing, to the pan and fry over a medium heat, turning them several times, for about 10 minutes, or according to the packet instructions.

2. Meanwhile, slice the garlic lengthways into 4 thin slices. Cut the tomato across into 4 slices. Cut the mozzarella cheese into 4 slices about the same size as the tomato slices.

3. Put 1 slice of garlic, 1 slice of tomato and finally 1 slice of mozzarella on top of each steaklet. Season to taste with salt and pepper. Cover and cook over a low heat for about 5 minutes, until the cheese begins to melt.

4. Transfer the steaklets to individual warm serving plates and garnish with the basil leaves. Serve immediately with a mixed salad and rustic bread.

Tip

This recipe would also work well with bacon steaks or slices of gammon.

Above: Baked steaklets
Below: Baked red cabbage with liver sausage

Tuna salad with white beans

Sweet lamb's lettuce, also known as mâche, is the perfect complement to tuna.

Easy

Serves 2
355 g/12 oz can tuna in brine
400 g/14 oz can haricot or
*   cannellini beans,*
1 onion
30 ml/2 tablespoons red
*   wine vinegar*
5 ml/1 teaspoon Dijon mustard
30 ml/2 tablespoons olive oil
50 g/2 oz black olives, stoned
salt and freshly ground black pepper
lamb's lettuce, to serve

Approximately per portion:
3,200 kJ/760 kcal
50 g protein, 45 g fat
27 g carbohydrate

● Approximate preparation
   time: 10 minutes

---

1. Thoroughly drain the tuna and the beans. Rinse the beans under cold running water.

2. Finely chop the onion. Flake the tuna with two forks.

3. Whisk together the vinegar, salt and pepper to taste and the mustard in a large bowl. Then beat in the oil until thoroughly mixed.

4 Add the onion, beans, tuna and olives and toss thoroughly to coat. Transfer to individual serving plates and serve with lamb's lettuce.

Tip

Instead of tuna, you can simply use the beans and 50 g/2 oz ewe's milk cheese.

Meatballs in tomato sauce

This is a quick and easy version of a classic Italian combination and, served with mashed potato and salad, is the ideal dish for a midweek supper.

Economical

Serves 2
50 g/2 oz streaky bacon slices
5 ml/1 teaspoon vegetable oil
1 onion
400 g/14 oz can tomatoes
5 ml/1 teaspoon dried oregano
300 g/11 oz frozen meatballs
2 portions instant mashed potato
salt and freshly ground
*   black pepper*
endive salad with yogurt and chive
*   dressing, to serve*

Approximately per portion:
2,900 kJ/690 kcal
28 g protein, 47 g fat
41 g carbohydrate

● Approximate preparation
   time: 20 minutes

---

1. Remove the rind from the bacon, if necessary, and cut the bacon into thin strips. Heat the oil in a saucepan. Add the bacon and fry over a medium heat.

2. Finely chop the onion. Add it to the pan and fry over a low heat until soft and translucent.

3. Add the tomatoes, together with their can juice, and break them up them with a fork. Season to taste with salt and pepper and stir in the oregano. Add the meatballs and simmer for 10–15 minutes

4. Meanwhile, prepare the mashed potato following the packet instructions.

5. Arrange the meatballs with the sauce and the mashed potato on warm individual serving plates. Serve with endive salad with a yogurt and chive dressing.

Tip

Fry the bacon and onion in the oil in the microwave for 3 minutes on HIGH. Add the tomatoes, meatballs, seasoning and oregano and cook for a further 6–7 minutes.

Above: Tuna salad with white beans
Below: Meatballs in tomato sauce

Orange mascarpone cream

Easy

Serves 2
1 large orange, about 250 g/9 oz
130 g/4¹/2 oz mascarpone
30 ml/2 tablespoons caster sugar
15 ml/1 tablespoon orange liqueur
15 ml/1 tablespoon chopped
*   pistachio nuts and 2 orange slices,*
*   to decorate*

Approximately per portion:
1,600 kJ/ 380 kcal
10 g protein, 25 g fat
28 g carbohydrate

● Approximate preparation
time: 15 minutes

---

1. Cut the orange in half and squeeze 1 half. Whisk together the orange juice, mascarpone, sugar and orange liqueur until the sugar has dissolved.

2. Cut the other orange half into slices and remove the peel and all traces of pith. Cut the flesh into bite-size chunks, removing the membrane and mix them into the mascarpone cream.

3. Spoon the cream into two chilled dessert dishes and sprinkle with chopped pistachio nuts.

Tip

This cream also tastes wonderful made with lemon or pink grapefruit.

Vanilla cream with mixed berries

You can use whatever combination of berries you like, such as raspberries, strawberries, blackberries or loganberries. You could substitute kirsch or crème de cassis for the brandy, but it is better to omit the alcohol if a child is eating with you.

Easy

Serves 2
300 g/11 oz mixed berries, frozen
*   or fresh*
30 ml/2 tablespoons orange brandy
*   or liqueur*
1 packet vanilla-flavoured
*   instant dessert*
300 ml/¹/2 pint cold milk
30 ml/2 tablespoons ground
*   almonds*
2 fresh mint sprigs,
*   to decorate*

Approximately per portion:
1,400 kJ/ 330 kcal
10 g protein, 17 g fat
31 g carbohydrate

● Approximate preparation
time: 15 minutes

---

1. Thaw the berries and mix them with the orange brandy.

2. Make the vanilla dessert with cold milk, following the packet instructions. Stir in the ground almonds. mixing thoroughly.

3. Put the berries into two sundae glasses and top them with the vanilla dessert. Garnish with the mint sprigs and serve.

Tip

You can also mix the berries with 250 g/9 oz Quark or other curd cheese or 200 ml/7 fl oz stiffly whipped double cream. Sweeten the cheese or cream with sugar, honey or fruit syrup to taste.

Above: Vanilla cream with mixed berries
Below: Orange mascarpone cream

Cherry bites with cinnamon sugar

If you serve a salad or soup for a starter, this delicious traditional dish is quite adequate as a sweet main course.

Economical

Serves 2
400 g/14 oz can morello cherries
130 g/4^{1}/2 oz plain flour
2 eggs
120 ml/4 fl oz milk
15 g/^{1}/2 oz butter
15 ml/1 tablespoon vegetable oil
30 ml/2 tablespoons caster sugar
5 ml/1 teaspoon cinnamon
salt

Approximately per portion:
2,400 kJ/570 kcal
16 g protein, 19 g fat
82 g carbohydrate

● Approximate preparation time: 20 minutes

---

1. Drain the cherries and reserve the can juice.

2. Sift the flour with a pinch of salt into a mixing bowl. Add the eggs and milk and whisk to a smooth batter. Stir in the reserved juice.

3. Heat the butter and the oil in a large, heavy-based frying pan. Pour in the batter and fry the pancake for about 5–6 minutes, until golden brown. Flip over and cook on the other side for 5–6 minutes. Then tear it up into medium-size pieces, using 2 forks. Add the cherries.

4. Mix the sugar and cinnamon in a small bowl. Arrange the cherry pancake pieces on two plates, sprinkle them with the cinnamon sugar and serve immediately.

Melon salad with ice cream

This dessert is very refreshing, which makes it especially suitable for hot summer days. Serve it with the ice cream of your choice.

Exquisite

Serves 2
1 small melon
1 kiwi fruit
30 ml/2 tablespoons clear honey
30 ml/2 tablespoons rum
30 ml/2 tablespoons sesame seeds
30 ml/2 tablespoons caster sugar
2 scoops of ice cream

Approximately per portion:
1,400 kJ/ 330 kcal
5 g protein, 8 g fat
53 g carbohydrate

● Approximate preparation time: 20 minutes

---

1. Cut the melon in half and scoop out the seeds with a spoon. Scoop out the flesh with a melon-baller and put the balls into a bowl.

2. Peel the kiwi fruit, quarter it lengthways and then slice the quarters across. Mix the kiwi slices with the melon balls.

3. Mix together the honey and rum in a small bowl, stirring until the honey has completely dissolved. Pour the rum mixture over the melon salad and set aside.

4. Meanwhile, put the sesame seeds into a non-stick frying pan. Sprinkle the castor sugar on to them and place over a medium heat, stirring constantly, until caramelized. Fold them into the melon salad.

5. Arrange the melon salad on two dessert plates and put a scoop of ice cream in the middle of each plate. Serve immediately.

Tip

If you have not got a melon-baller, you can cut the melon into eighths. Then remove the skin and cut up the flesh into neat dice with a sharp knife. If the melon is a very soft-fleshed variety, you can scoop out balls using a teaspoon.

Above: Cherry bites with cinnamon sugar
Below: Melon salad with ice cream

Fruit parcels

Exquisite

Serves 2
1 banana
1 apple
1 orange
15 ml/1 tablespoon caster sugar
30 ml/2 tablespoons orange liqueur
15 ml/1 tablespoon flaked almonds
5 ml/1 teaspoon butter
whipped cream, to serve

Approximately per portion:
890 kJ/210 kcal
3 g protein, 7 g fat
32 g carbohydrate

● Approximate preparation
  time: 25 minutes

1. Preheat the oven to 240°C/ 475°F/Gas 9. Peel the banana and cut it into slices. Quarter and core the apple and cut it into wedges. Peel the orange and remove all the pith. Cut it into segments, removing the membranes.

2. Put the fruit into a bowl and add the sugar, liqueur and almonds and mix thoroughly.

3. Cut 2 pieces of foil and grease with the butter. Divide the fruit between them. Wrap each piece of foil up into a parcel and bake the fruit in the oven for about 10 minutes.

4. Take out the foil packets and just open the top. Transfer the parcels to two plates and serve with whipped cream.

Tip

Of course, you can use other fruits. Try pineapple or peaches.

Avocado cream with coconut

Exquisite

Serves 2
30 ml/2 tablespoons desiccated
* coconut*
30 ml/2 tablespoons clear honey
250 g/9 oz Quark or other
* curd cheese*
I ripe avocado
juice of ¹/₂ lemon

Approximately per portion:
2,200 kJ/520 kcal
16 g protein, 40 g fat
29 g carbohydrate

● Approximate preparation
  time: 15 minutes

1. Dry-fry the coconut in a non-stick pan until golden brown. Set aside to cool.

2. Mix the honey with the cheese.

3. Cut the avocado in half and remove the stone. Scoop out the flesh with a spoon. Process the flesh, together with the lemon juice, in a food processor. Stir the avocado purée into the cheese and honey mixture.

4. Reserve 10 ml/2 teaspoons of the coconut and stir the remainder into the cheese mixture. Put the avocado cream into individual dishes and sprinkle with the reserved coconut.

Tip

This dessert tastes even more delicious if it is made with grated fresh coconut.

Cream cheese and apricot tartlets

You can easily make these little fruit tartlets for more than two people. They are quick to make and therefore perfect for unexpected guests.

Easy

Serves 2
400 g/14 oz can apricot halves in juice
200 g/7 oz full-fat cream cheese
45 ml/3 tablespoons caster sugar
1–2 drops vanilla essence
45 ml/3 tablespoons chopped pistachio nuts
4 ready-made tartlet cases or individual flan cases

For 4 tartlets, approximately per tartlet:
1,440 kJ/335 kcal
9 g protein, 20 g fat
30 g carbohydrate

● Approximate preparation time: 10 minutes

I. Drain the apricots and reserve the juice.

2. Put the cream cheese into a bowl. Add the sugar and vanilla essence and mix thoroughly.

3. Stir in about 60 ml/ 4 tablespoons of the reserved apricot juice. The mixture should be creamy and smooth. If it seems too thick, add a little more apricot juice, but do not make it runny.

4. Sprinkle in half the pistachio nuts and mix together.

5. Spread the tartlet cases evenly with the cream cheese mixture. Top with the apricot halves and sprinkle with the remaining pistachio nuts.

Tip

You can also use fresh, stoned apricots. In that case, mix some fruit liqueur or fruit juice into the cream cheese.

Golden rice

This desert also tastes very good when served cold.

Economical

Serves 2
130 g/4 1/2 oz easy-cook rice
2 eggs
45 ml/3 tablespoons caster sugar
1–2 drops vanilla essence
250 g/9 oz Quark or other curd cheese
5 ml/1 teaspoon ground cinnamon
30 ml/2 tablespoons chopped blanched almonds
30 ml/2 tablespoons raisins
butter, for greasing
salt

Approximately per portion:
2,600 kJ/620 kcal
30 g protein, 21 g fat
85 g carbohydrate

● Approximate preparation time: 30 minutes

I. Bring a large saucepan of lightly salted water to the boil. Add the rice and cook, following the packet instructions. Drain thoroughly. Preheat the oven to 220°C/425°F/ Gas 7.

2. Put the eggs, caster sugar and vanilla essence into a bowl and beat with the whisk attachment of a hand-held electric mixer until pale and fluffy.

3. Stir in the cheese, add the cinnamon, almonds and raisins and mix thoroughly.

4. Grease an ovenproof dish with butter. Mix the drained rice with the cheese and spoon into the prepared dish. Bake in the oven for about 15 minutes.

Tip

Vanilla sugar is easy to make and a useful store-cupboard stand-by. Empty 450 g/1 lb caster sugar into a large airtight container and add 1 vanilla pod. Within a week, the sugar will have acquired the flavour of vanilla. You can continue to top up the sugar for several months before it is necessary to replace the vanilla pod.

Above: Golden rice
Below: Cream cheese and apricot tartlets

Great Little Cook Books
Cooking for Two

Published originally under the title
Für Zwei schnell und gut! by Gräfe
und Unzer Verlag GmbH,
München

© 1997 by Gräfe und Unzer Verlag
GmbH, München

English-language edition
© 1999 by Transedition Limited,
Oxford, England

This edition published in 2001
by Advanced Marketing,
Bicester, Oxfordshire.

Translation:
Translate-A-Book, Oxford

Editing:
Linda Doeser

Typesetting:
Organ Graphic, Abingdon

10 9 8 7 6 5 4 3
Printed in Dubai

ISBN 1 901683 22 2

Front cover illustration: You will
find the recipe for Prawns in
saffron cream on page 34.

Note:
For all recipes, ingredients are
given in metric and imperial
measurements. Follow only one
set, as they are not
interchangeable.

Cornelia Adam
initially worked as a professional
hotel keeper. Later, she took her
wide experience abroad on
professional trips as the editor of a
famous illustrated women's
magazine. For some time now, she
has worked as a freelance food
journalist and cookery book writer.

Odette Teubner
was taught by her father, the
internationally renowned food
photographer, Christian Teubner.
She then worked for some months
as a fashion photographer. At
present, she works exclusively in
the Teubner Studio for Food
Photography. In her spare time, she
is an enthusiastic painter of
children's portraits, using her own
son as a model.

Dorothee Gödert
After finishing her studies in
photography, she started work as a
photographer of still life and
interiors. After spending some
time in Princeton in the United
States, she specialized in food
photography. She has worked with
a number of well-known food
photographers and now works in
the Teubner Studio for Food
Photography.